# Botanical Hearts

## DESIGNS COLORING BOOK
FOR ADULTS

Coloring Therapists
STRESS RELIEVING COLORING ACTIVITIES

Coloring Therapists LLC
40 E. Main St. #1156
Newark, DE 19711
*www.coloringtherapists.com*

***This is a Bleed Through Page If You Are Using a Coloring Marker or Pen!***

*Find Other Great Titles By searching for Coloring Therapists on Your Favorite Book Retailer*

**Amazon.Com | Barnes & Noble (BN.Com) | Books A Million (BAM.Com)**

Coloring Therapists

STRESS RELIEVING COLORING ACTIVITIES

***This is a Bleed Through Page If You Are Using a Coloring Marker or Pen!***
*Find Other Great Titles By searching for Coloring Therapists on Your Favorite Book Retailer*
**Amazon.Com | Barnes & Noble (BN.Com) | Books A Million (BAM.Com)**

Coloring Therapists
STRESS RELIEVING COLORING ACTIVITIES

SPRING

***This is a Bleed Through Page If You Are Using a Coloring Marker or Pen!***
*Find Other Great Titles By searching for Coloring Therapists on Your Favorite Book Retailer*
**Amazon.Com | Barnes & Noble (BN.Com) | Books A Million (BAM.Com)**

***This is a Bleed Through Page If You Are Using a Coloring Marker or Pen!***

*Find Other Great Titles By searching for Coloring Therapists on Your Favorite Book Retailer*

**Amazon.Com | Barnes & Noble (BN.Com) | Books A Million (BAM.Com)**

Coloring Therapists

STRESS RELIEVING COLORING ACTIVITIES

***This is a Bleed Through Page If You Are Using a Coloring Marker or Pen!***

*Find Other Great Titles By searching for Coloring Therapists on Your Favorite Book Retailer*

**Amazon.Com | Barnes & Noble (BN.Com) | Books A Million (BAM.Com)**

***This is a Bleed Through Page If You Are Using a Coloring Marker or Pen!***

*Find Other Great Titles By searching for Coloring Therapists on Your Favorite Book Retailer*

**Amazon.Com | Barnes & Noble (BN.Com) | Books A Million (BAM.Com)**

Love

***This is a Bleed Through Page If You Are Using a Coloring Marker or Pen!***

*Find Other Great Titles By searching for Coloring Therapists on Your Favorite Book Retailer*

**Amazon.Com | Barnes & Noble (BN.Com) | Books A Million (BAM.Com)**

Coloring Therapists

STRESS RELIEVING COLORING ACTIVITIES

***This is a Bleed Through Page If You Are Using a Coloring Marker or Pen!***

*Find Other Great Titles By searching for Coloring Therapists on Your Favorite Book Retailer*

**Amazon.Com | Barnes & Noble (BN.Com) | Books A Million (BAM.Com)**

CT

Coloring Therapists

STRESS RELIEVING COLORING ACTIVITIES

***This is a Bleed Through Page If You Are Using a Coloring Marker or Pen!***

*Find Other Great Titles By searching for Coloring Therapists on Your Favorite Book Retailer*

**Amazon.Com | Barnes & Noble (BN.Com) | Books A Million (BAM.Com)**

***This is a Bleed Through Page If You Are Using a Coloring Marker or Pen!***

*Find Other Great Titles By searching for Coloring Therapists on Your Favorite Book Retailer*

**Amazon.Com | Barnes & Noble (BN.Com) | Books A Million (BAM.Com)**

***This is a Bleed Through Page If You Are Using a Coloring Marker or Pen!***

*Find Other Great Titles By searching for Coloring Therapists on Your Favorite Book Retailer*

**Amazon.Com | Barnes & Noble (BN.Com) | Books A Million (BAM.Com)**